THE ZACK FILES™

Great-Grandpa's in the Litter Box

THE ZACK FILES™

Great-Grandpa's in the Litter Box

by Dan Greenburg
Illustrated by Jack E. Davis

Long tail Books

Great-Grandpa's in the Litter Box

First published in the United States by Grosset & Dunlap, Inc., a member of Penguin Putnam Books for Young Readers under the title GREAT-GRANDPA'S IN THE LITTER BOX.

This Korean and English edition was published by Longtail Books, Inc. in 2020 by arrangement with Sheldon Fogelman Agency, Inc. through KCC(Korea Copyright Center Inc.), Seoul.

ISBN 979-11-86701-54-6 14740

Longtail Books

I'd like to thank my editors,
Jane O'Connor and Judy Donnelly,
who make the process of writing and revising
so much fun, and without whom
these books would not exist.

I also want to thank
Jennifer Dussling and Laura Driscoll
for their terrific ideas.

For Judith, and for the real Zack,

with love—D.G.

Chapter 1

My name is Zack. I'm ten years old and I guess you could say I've been interested in **weird stuff** all my life. Stuff like **haunt**ed houses, UFOs,[1] and **storm**s where it rains frogs. So when something weird happened to me, I was probably more **open-minded**

1 **UFO** (= Unidentified Flying Object) 미확인 비행물체. 전문가의 눈이나 전파 탐지 등으로도 정체를 탐지할 수 없는 비행체를 말한다.

than somebody else who wasn't interested in weird stuff all their life.

I was in the animal **shelter** near our home in New York City. After years of **beg**ging my dad for a cat, he finally **broke down** and said yes. I could get a **kitten**. So here I was.

I passed a **cage** with an old gray **tomcat** inside it. His **fur** was **matted** with **dirt**. He'd lost half the **whisker**s on the left side of his face, which made him look a little **lopsided**. And the **tip** had been **chew**ed off of one of his ears.

"Sssst! Young man!" Someone was calling me. The voice sounded **raspy** and strange. "Hello, little boy! Over here!"

I turned around, looking to see who it

was. But there was nobody in **sight**.

I went on to a cage where a little tuxedo[2] kitten with a black body and white **paw**s was taking a **nap**. He sure was cute. I stopped to take a closer look at him. Of course, it probably wasn't the best time for me to **adopt** a kitten. In a couple of days my dad and I were flying to Chicago to spend Thanksgiving[3] with my Grandma Leah. But our **neighbor** had agreed to cat-sit.[4] And I wasn't **taking** any **chance**s of my dad changing his mind.

I'd almost decided on that cute little

---

2 **tuxedo** 마치 턱시도 코트를 입은 것처럼 하얀색과 검은색이 섞인 털을 지닌 고양이를 가리키는 표현.

3 **Thanksgiving** 추수감사절. 북미 지역의 전통적 명절이자 국경일로 이날 칠면조 구이를 먹는 풍습이 있다.

4 **cat-sit** 'baby-sit(아기를 봐 주다)'라는 말에 'baby' 대신 'cat'을 넣어서 사용한 표현으로 '고양이를 봐 주다'라는 뜻이다.

tuxedo kitten when I heard the voice again:

"Hey, kid," said the voice. "I am *speaking* to you."

"Where are you?" I asked.

"Right here, **dummy**," said the voice. "In the cage in back of you."

I turned around. That **scruffy** old gray tomcat was **staring** quite **cross**ly at me.

"You'll **pardon** me for **holler**ing," said the cat. "But I was afraid you **were about to** make a terrible mistake and choose somebody else."

"You can *talk!*" I said, **hardly** able to **believe my ears**.

I moved closer to his cage. I wanted to see if his cat **lip**s moved when he talked.

Maybe this was just a **trick**—somebody doing ventriloquism.[5] I mean I told you I like weird stuff, but this was really **far out**, even for me. "A talking cat?" I said.

"Yeah, a talking cat, how about that," said the cat **sarcastic**ally.

His cat lips were moving! This was no trick!

"But look at you—a talking boy," he said. "Listen, we don't have much time. You've got to get me out of here."

"What do you mean?"

"I mean I can't **stand** it in here a minute longer," he said. "The **meow**ing and the smell are **driving** me right **up the wall**.

---

5 **ventriloquism** 복화술. 입을 움직이지 않고 말하는 기술. 주로 인형을 가지고 공연을 할 때, 인형이 말하는 것처럼 보이게 하는 데 사용한다.

Tell them you're adopting me."

"Uh, I don't mean to hurt your feelings," I said. "But I've already decided on this little tuxedo kitten here." Like I said before, I'm pretty open-minded. I had nothing against talking cats. I just wasn't sure I wanted to live with one. Especially with one as **bossy** as this one seemed.

"The tuxedo kitten?" he said. "Poor choice."

"What do you mean?"

"He has **flea**s and **worm**s. Plus he never **got the hang of** using a **litter** box."

The tomcat gave me a long look. He could see I wasn't **buy**ing it.

"OK," the cat **went on**. "I didn't want to have to use this. But here goes: If you don't adopt me, they're going to **put** me **to sleep**. And I don't mean **tuck** me in bed in my **jammies** either. I mean kill me. You really want that on your **conscience**, kid?"

"Listen, they don't put cats to sleep here," I said. "That is a **well-known** fact." This cat was not only bossy, he also seemed to have problems with the truth.

"OK, I **admit** they haven't lately," he said. "But that could change any day."

I looked at him and shook my head.

"OK, OK," he said. "How's about this: What if I told you I know your name?"

"What's my name?"

"Zack."

"How—how did you know that?" I asked. I had to admit I was pretty

impressed. Not that many people know my name, and even fewer cats.

"You're impressed, huh?" said the big gray tomcat. "What if I told you I'm a member of your family, Zack? Do you think you'd still prefer the little tuxedo?"

"A member of my *family?*" I said. "How could that be? You're a cat."

"Hey, you never heard of **reincarnation**? Somebody dies and comes back as somebody else?"

"So?" I said. Sure, I'd heard of reincarnation. In fact, I'd read about several cases in India of kids who **claim**ed to have lived before. They knew facts about certain places they'd never been, things they couldn't possibly have known if they were **ordinary** kids. Still, they were kids, not cats. "So what?"

"So," said the gray tomcat, "I happen to be your wonderful dead Great-Grandfather Julius."

Chapter 2

One minute I'**m about to** go home with a cute little black-and-white **kitten**, the next a big gray **tomcat** tells me he's my dead great-grandfather. I didn't know what to do. I took another look at the kitten. He was **lick**ing his front **paw** in an **adorable** way. The tomcat saw I was still **lean**ing **toward** the kitten.

"What? You don't think I'm cute?" he asked. Then he **pose**d in what he must have thought was a cute pose.

"You're . . . *kind* of cute, sir," I said. "It's just that . . ."

"Cute, shmute,[1]" he said. "You can't tell me you're going to walk out of here with a **flea-bitten** stranger who hasn't been **proper**ly **toilet-train**ed and leave your **beloved** great-grandfather **rot**ting in a **stink**ing little **cage**? Family is family, Zack."

I looked at the tomcat, then at the kitten, then at the tomcat. *Family is family*. Funny, that's something Grandma Leah always

1 **shm-** 접두사로 단어의 앞에 붙여 무시하거나 경멸하는 뜻이 담긴 표현을 만들 수 있다.

says. That did it.

"I guess you're right, sir," I said. "I guess family is family."

"Now you're **talk**ing **sense**, kid," said the cat. "And, please, call me Great-Grandpa Julius."

Chapter 3

When I arrived home, **huffing and puffing**, carrying my cardboard[1] cat **carrier**, my dad met me at the door. Since my parents **split** up, I live part of the time with my dad and part with my mom.

"So," he said, smiling, "it looks like

1 **cardboard** 판지. 두껍고 단단하게 만든 종이.

you've finally gotten yourself a **kitty**."

"Yeah," I said, and put the cat carrier down. I was **exhaust**ed. With Great-Grandpa Julius inside it, it must have **weigh**ed close to thirty pounds.[2]

"Can I see the little guy?" asked my dad.

"Sure, Dad," I said. "But first I have to tell you a couple of things."

"OK, what?"

"Well, number one, I didn't get a kitten. I got a **slight**ly older cat."

"Why,[3] Zack," said my dad, "I think that's a wonderful thing to do, giving an

---

2 **pound** 무게의 단위 파운드. 1파운드는 약 0.45킬로그램이다. (30파운드는 약 13.6킬로그램이다.)

3 **why** 여기에서는 이유를 묻거나 말할 때 쓰는 의문사 또는 관계사가 아닌 '어머', '아니'라는 뜻의 감탄사로 쓰였다.

older cat a home. I'm very proud of you, son."

"Uh-huh. And number two, he's not an **ordinary** cat, Dad. He's . . . well, for one thing, he talks."

"He talks," said my dad.

"Yeah, he talks."

My dad smiled, deciding to **go along with** my little **joke**.

"I see. Well, what does he say?"

"He says he's Great-Grandpa Julius."

"I didn't even think you remembered having a Great-Grandpa Julius," he said, **chuckling**.

What I remembered was hearing Grandma Leah **go on** about her father, Julius, who was so nice he was **practical**ly a **saint**. Then she'd always add how Julius was the complete **opposite** of Great-Grandpa Maurice, her husband's father. Maurice was the **black sheep** of the family.

So far, Julius didn't seem that saintly to me. I opened the cat carrier. Great-Grandpa Julius and my dad took a good long look at each other.

"Well, he's certainly . . . big," said my dad. "Hello, Great-Grandpa Julius. Remember me? Dan? You always used to say I was your favorite grandchild. Can you say hello?"

Great-Grandpa Julius seemed **about to** say something. Then he **scratch**ed behind his ear with his **hind** leg instead.

"He's not very **talkative**," said my dad.

"You should have heard him at the animal **shelter**," I said.

My dad chuckled and walked off, shaking his head.

"How come you didn't talk to my dad?" I asked.

"I talk when I want to," said the cat, "not when other people want me to. Hey, Zack, you got anything to eat around here? I'm so hungry I could eat **rodent**s."

I had the free can of cat food they gave me at the animal shelter. I put it into a **bowl** on the floor. Great-Grandpa Julius **sniff**ed it and **wrinkle**d up his nose.

"Feh!" he said. "What *is* that **stuff**?"

"Beef **by-product**s in gravy,[4]" I replied.

"You got maybe a little herring[5] with sour cream?[6]"

I told him we didn't have anything like that. He did not take this at all well.

"Let's put it this way, kid," said Great-Grandpa Julius. "Either get me some herring with sour cream **pronto**, or I'm going to take a **leak** on your sofa."

"You're not serious about this," I said.

"Try me," he said.

If you ask me, Great-Grandpa Julius was a lot **crankier** than I'd heard. But I was trying to be understanding. I guess dying

---

4 **gravy** 그레이비. 고기를 익힐 때 나온 육즙에 밀가루 등을 넣어 만든 소스.

5 **herring** 청어. 청어과의 바닷물고기로 등은 짙은 청색이고, 배는 은백색인 등 푸른 생선의 한 종류이다.

6 **sour cream** 사워크림. 생크림을 발효시켜 만든 새콤한 맛이 나는 크림.

and getting **reincarnate**d as a cat could **spoil** a person's **mood**.

Chapter 4

Luckily, the **deli** on the corner sold herring with sour cream. I brought it back to Great-Grandpa Julius.

"Now you're talking,[1]" he said when he saw it. He **gobble**d it up. "Not bad. Not bad at all. But tomorrow, Zack, be sure

1 **now you are talking** 다른 사람이 하는 말에 동의하거나 찬성할 때 쓰는 표현으로 '바로 그거야!' 또는 '그거 좋은 생각이야!'라는 뜻이다.

the deli man doesn't **skimp** on the sour cream."

Boy,[2] this cat was **pushy**!

"Listen, I can't buy you herring and sour cream every day," I said. "I only get three dollars a week **allowance**. And I won't be able to buy it for you over Thanksgiving weekend—I won't even be here. I'm going to Chicago. To visit Grandma Leah."

"We're going to visit Leah?" he asked **delighted**ly.

"*I* am," I said. "You're staying here with a **neighbor**."

"You'd go to Chicago and you wouldn't take me to see my own daughter? If Leah

---

2 **boy** 여기에서는 '소년'이라는 뜻이 아니라, '맙소사!' 또는 '어머나!'라는 의미로 놀람이나 실망, 기쁨 등을 나타내는 표현으로 쓰였다.

heard I was reincarnated and didn't come to see her, she'd be **crush**ed."

"Well," I said, "let me ask my dad."

"Zack," said my dad, "I'm **willing** to **go along with** a **joke**. But we both know cats can't talk. Although I must **admit** I'm **tempt**ed to bring him to Chicago, just to see the expression on Grandma Leah's face when you tell her that cat is her father."

"Dad, I'd really like to take him to Chicago. I think it would mean a lot to him."

"I'll tell you what," said my dad. "If you can get him to talk to me, you can take him to Chicago."

I went back to my room, where Great-

Grandpa Julius was **paw**ing through my **collection** of baseball cards.

"You have any cards with Lou Gehrig,[3] Ty Cobb,[4] or Rogers Hornsby[5] on them?" he asked.

"No, I'm afraid not."

"Gehrig and Hornsby were nice **fella**s. Cobb not so nice."

"That's what I hear."

"But all three **sign**ed my baseball."

"You're saying you actually met Lou Gehrig, Ty Cobb, and Rogers Hornsby?" I

---

3 **Lou Gehrig** 루 게릭. 뉴욕 양키스(New York Yankees)팀에서 4번 타자로 활약한 미국의 프로 야구 선수. 근육 위축증으로 사망하여, 이 병에 그의 이름이 별명으로 붙었다.

4 **Ty Cobb** 타이 코브 또는 타이러스 코브(Tyrus Cobb). 디트로이트 타이거스(Detroit Tigers)팀에서 외야수로 활약한 미국의 프로 야구 선수.

5 **Rogers Hornsby** 로저스 혼즈비. 미국의 프로 야구 선수, 코치이자 감독. 메이저리그 역사상 가장 위대한 타자들 가운데 한 사람으로 손꼽힌다.

said. The **tomcat nod**ded. "What happened to the ball they signed?"

"I have it."

"Where?"

"In a safe place, don't worry about it. So did your dad say I could come to Chicago?"

"He said on one **condition**."

"What's that?"

"You have to talk to him. I don't think he believes you can talk."

"That's all I have to do, talk to him?"

"That's all."

"OK, let's do it."

I followed Great-Grandpa Julius, who **pad**ded into the living room, where my dad was reading the newspaper.

"Dad," I said, "Great-Grandpa Julius has something to say to you."

"Really?" said my dad. He put down his paper and turned toward the cat, with a big smile on his face. "All right," he said. "Tell me. What was the hardest part about changing from a person into a cat?"

Great-Grandpa Julius looked at my dad a moment without speaking. Then he **cock**ed his head, opened his mouth, and said, "For me, I guess the hardest part was finding out there wasn't a door you could **lock** behind you on the **litter** box. Is that good enough for a trip to Chicago?"

My dad's eyes looked like they were going to **pop** right out of his head.

"Sounds good enough to me," I said.

"How about you, Dad?"

Chapter 5

Once my dad found out my cat was Great-Grandpa Julius, he kept asking him questions about what it was like being dead. Dad never **let up** for the two days before we left for Chicago, and all during the long **ride** to the airport.

"Some people who died and were brought back to life again **claim** they went through what looked like a very long **tunnel** with very bright light at the other end," said my dad. "And all their dead **relative**s met them on the other side. Did that happen to you?"

"I do remember going through a long tunnel and coming out to bright light on the other side," said Great-Grandpa Julius from inside his cat carrying case.

"You do?" said my dad excitedly.

"Yes," said Great-Grandpa Julius. "It happened to be the Midtown Tunnel.[1] And the bright light on the other side was Queens.[2] That's where they **buried** me.

---

1 **Midtown Tunnel** 미드타운 터널. 뉴욕시의 이스트강(East River) 아래에 놓인 터널로, 맨해튼(Manhattan)과 퀸스(Queens), 두 자치구를 연결한다.

2 **Queens** 퀸스. 미국 뉴욕주(州) 뉴욕시에 속한 다섯 개의 자치구 가운데 하나.

Tell me something. Would you happen to have a cigar[3] on you? It's been years since I've smoked a really good cigar."

"You should stop smoking cigars," I said. "They're bad for you."

"I guess you're right," said Great-Grandpa Julius. "But some things you just don't stop **craving**, even after you're dead."

"How long have you been a cat?" asked my dad.

"I don't have a driver's **license** on me," said Great-Grandpa Julius. "How old do I look?"

"About twelve or thirteen," I said.

---

3 **cigar** 시가. 담뱃잎을 썰지 않고 통째로 돌돌 말아서 만든 담배.

"That feels about right," he said. "Of course, I didn't come back as a cat right away."

"You didn't?"

"Oh no. First I was a **caterpillar**."

"A caterpillar?" I said. "What was that like?"

"**Extreme**ly boring. Mostly it was about eating leaves. I ate leaves and tried to pretend they were herring with sour cream. Say,[4] you wouldn't **by any chance** happen to have a little schnapps[5] on you?"

"What's schnapps?" I asked.

"**Liquor**," said my dad. "No, I'm sorry, I

---

4 **say** 말을 처음 꺼낼 때 쓰는 표현으로 '저', '글쎄' 또는 '그러니까'라는 뜻이다.

5 **schnapps** 슈냅스. 곡식이나 감자 등으로 만든 독하고 색이 없으며 다양한 향을 내는 술.

don't carry schnapps on me."

We arrived at the airport. Dad paid the **cab** driver. I tried to put Great-Grandpa Julius back into his cat **carrier**.

"Hey, c'mon," he cried. "Don't make me travel in a **suitcase** again. I'm a **dignified** old **geezer**, for Pete's **sake**."

"In a past life you were a dignified old geezer," I said. "In *this* life you're a **stray** cat. And cats travel in cat carriers."

Julius **sigh**ed and got into his carrier.

Once we got on the plane, Dad started in again with his questions.

"So, Julius," said Dad, "after you were a caterpillar, did you become a butterfly?"

"No, a **moth**," said the voice inside the cat carrier. "Mostly that was about eating

sweaters."

"You ate sweaters?" I said. "Ugh!"

"Don't **knock** it till you've tried it," said Great-Grandpa Julius. "I remember one fine cashmere[6] turtleneck.[7] It was almost as **tasty** as a corned beef[8] on **rye**. Then one night I happened to fly a little too close to a **torch** outside a Polynesian[9] restaurant and—pffft!"

"Another tunnel?"

"No, no, moths don't get tunnels. Only humans get tunnels. After that I became a

---

6 **cashmere** 캐시미어. 인도의 카슈미르(Kashmir) 지방에서 나는 산양의 털로 짠 고급 모직물. 부드럽고 윤기가 있으며, 보온성이 좋다.

7 **turtleneck** 긴 목 부분을 접어서 입는 스웨터.

8 **corned beef** 콘드 비프. 소고기를 소금이나 향신료 등에 절이고 쪄서 통조림으로 만든 것.

9 **Polynesian** '폴리네시아의'라는 뜻. 폴리네시아는 태평양 중·남부에 펼쳐 있는 여러 섬을 통틀어 이르는 말이다.

mouse."

"And that was all about eating cheese, I **suppose**," said my dad.

"No, about eating wood. Don't ask."

"Wait a minute," I said. "First you were a caterpillar, then you were a moth, then a mouse. How did you have time to be all those things?"

"We're not talking about a lot of time here," said Great-Grandpa Julius. "You could die, **do a stretch** as a caterpillar, then a moth, then a mouse, and you could still be back by a week from Thursday. But time didn't **matter** to me. I was dead. I had quite a lot of **leisure** time on my hands."

"Excuse me," said the **flight attendant**

as she passed our **row**. "In preparation for **takeoff**, please make sure your seat belts are **secure**ly **fasten**ed and that your seat backs and **tray** tables are in the **upright** and **lock**ed position."

"Hey, cookie,[10]" said Great-Grandpa Julius, "what are you doing after the flight?"

The flight attendant thought my dad said that, because she **gave** him **a dirty look**.

Then we **buckle**d up. Next stop—Chicago!

---

10 cookie 보통 귀여운 아이나 애인에게 애정을 담아 부르는 말.

Chapter 6

"Before we see her, I just want to ask you one thing," said my dad in the elevator of the building on Lake **Shore** Drive where Grandma Leah lives.

"What's that?" I asked.

"Grandma Leah is in her eighties. Do you really think it's safe to tell a woman in her eighties that her dead father is now a cat?"

"Grandma Leah is a very **peppy**, **open-minded** person," I replied. "I'm sure she'll take the news OK."

The elevator doors opened on the seventh floor and we walked down the **hall** to Grandma Leah's apartment, my dad carrying our **luggage** and me carrying the carrier with Great-Grandpa Julius in it.

Grandma Leah was so happy to see us. She kept hugging and kissing us all over the place. When we were all **settle**d in her apartment she **notice**d the cat carrier for the first time.

"Don't tell me you brought an animal all the way to Chicago?" she said.

"Not just any animal, Grandma," I said. "A very special animal."

"Special in what way?" asked Grandma Leah.

"Special in the way that he is not only a cat, he is also a member of our family," I said.

"**In other words**, you love him so much you feel he's a member of our family?" asked Grandma Leah.

I looked at my dad and then back at Grandma Leah.

"No," I said, "I mean he really is a member of our family."

And with that I opened up the cat carrier. Grandma Leah and Great-Grandpa Julius took their first look at each other.

"Grandma Leah," I said, "I believe this is your father, Great-Grandpa Julius."

Grandma Leah **stare**d at the cat in silence for a moment and then shook her head.

"No," she said. "I don't believe it is. My father was taller."

"Leah **dear**," said Great-Grandpa Julius, "it's so wonderful to see you again. How have you been all these years, my **darling**?"

"It's talking to me," said Grandma Leah in a very strange voice. "A cat is talking to me in the English language."

"He is," I said.

"Leah dear," said Great-Grandpa Julius, "I may be a cat, but I'm also your father."

"It's still talking to me," said Grandma Leah. "Am I right about this, that the cat is still talking to me?"

"You're right," I said.

"Tell the cat I said it's not my father," she said.

"Why don't you tell him yourself?" I suggested.

"I don't talk to cats," said Grandma Leah in the same strange voice.

"Grandma Leah says you're not her father," I said.

"I *heard* her, I *heard* her," said Great-Grandpa Julius. "What am I, **deaf**?" Then the cat **soften**ed his voice. "Leah dear, don't you remember me? It's Daddy!"

"Tell the cat I said that we never called

my father by the name of Daddy," said Grandma Leah. "Ask it what we called my real father."

"She says what name did she call you?" I asked.

"I heard her, I heard her." Great-Grandpa Julius's voice was rising. "You don't have to repeat everything she says."

"Well then, what name did she call you?"

"It wasn't Daddy," said Great-Grandpa Julius.

"We've already heard her say it wasn't Daddy," said my dad.

"Of course it wasn't Daddy," said Great-Grandpa Julius. "Because it was . . . Father."

Grandma Leah shook her head.

"Tell the cat it wasn't Father," said Grandma Leah.

"She says it wasn't—"

"Don't repeat it!" **snap**ped Great-Grandpa Julius angrily. Then he quickly **recover**ed his **composure**. "It wasn't Father. Of course it wasn't Father," he said. "Father was what I called myself. What you called me was . . . Papa."

"Tell the cat it wasn't Papa," said Grandma Leah.

"Oh boy," said Great-Grandpa Julius. "Could I ever use a good cigar or a glass of schnapps right about now. Leah dear, I'm over a hundred years old. I've been a **caterpillar**, a **moth**, a mouse. I've died many times, so my memory isn't quite what it used to be. Could you please **give** me **a break** here and tell me what you used to call me?"

"**Go on**, Grandma Leah," I said. "Tell him what you used to call him."

"I didn't call the *cat* anything," she said. "I called my *father*—my real father, my human father—Poppy."

"Poppy, shmoppy," said Great-Grandpa Julius. He **wave**d his **paw dismissive**ly. "How **far** is Poppy **from** Papa?"

"Wait a minute," said Grandma Leah. "I just **realize**d something."

"What's that?" I said.

"Did the cat say it wanted a good cigar or a glass of schnapps?"

"That's what he said," I said.

"My father, Julius, never smoked cigars. And he never drank schnapps. You know who smoked cigars and drank schnapps?"

"Who?" I said.

"Who?" said my dad.

"The **black sheep** of the family, that's who. Your cat is a liar, Zack. He's not my father, Julius, at all. He's your grandpa's **no-good** father. He's Great-Grandpa Maurice!"

Chapter 7

"Is what Grandma Leah says true?" I **demand**ed of the large gray **tomcat**. "Are you my grandpa's **no-good** father, Maurice?"

"Now, **hold your horses**, sonny, hold your horses," he said. "First of all, where does she **get off** calling me a no-good?"

"Where do I get off?" said Grandma

Leah angrily. "I'll tell you where I get off. You took thirty thousand dollars of my father's money to **work on** your crazy **invent**ions. Then you left town. **Disappear**ed. We never heard a word from you again."

We all turned to the cat.

"What inventions?" I asked.

"I'll tell you what inventions," said Grandma Leah. "A **hairpiece** for **bald** eagles[1] was one."

"Who would ever buy a hairpiece for bald eagles?" I asked the cat.

"Well, that was a problem," said the cat.

1 **bald eagle** 흰머리수리. 북미 대륙에서 볼 수 있는 덩치가 매우 큰 맹금류로 미국을 상징하는 새이다. 머리에 난 흰 털 때문에 대머리처럼 보인다고 해서 대머리수리라고도 부른다.

"Then there was the dog **whistle**," Grandma Leah **went on**. "Only dogs **were supposed to** be able to hear it."

"That sounds better," I said.

"**Except** for one little thing," she said. The cat looked **embarrass**ed. "Dogs could not hear it either. You **blew** it and all the mice in the **neighbor**hood came running."

"Did you invent anything that worked?" I asked.

"Yes!" said the cat. "A sweater for dachshunds[2] in the shape of a hot dog[3] **bun**. Very cute, if I do say so myself. At first it didn't sell. I thought I'd lost

---

2 **dachshund** 닥스훈트. 허리가 길고 다리가 짧은 개.

3 **hot dog** 길쭉한 빵을 세로로 갈라 뜨거운 소시지 등을 안에 넣고 케첩이나 겨자 소스 등을 바른 음식.

all of Julius's money, so I **beat it** out of town. But you know what? After a while that sweater started selling like crazy. Everybody who owned a dachshund had to have one. I made back the whole thirty thousand. I had it sent directly to a secret bank **account** in Chicago."

"A secret bank account?" I said.

"In the Morton F. Acropolis Savings and **Loan Association**[4] of Chicago," said the cat. "I was coming to Chicago to pay Julius back when I got hit by a Greyhound bus.[5]"

We all **stare**d at the cat.

---

4 **savings and loan association** 우리나라의 상호 저축 은행에 해당하는 미국의 지역 금융 기관. 주로 주택 담보 대출을 운영한다.

5 **Greyhound bus** 그레이하운드 버스. 미국 전역과 캐나다 및 멕시코 일부 도시를 연결하는 많은 노선을 지닌 미국의 장거리 버스 회사 및 그 버스.

"Great-Grandpa Maurice," I said gently. "You've told us many things that weren't true. How do we know what you're telling us now is the truth?"

"First thing tomorrow morning," he said, "take me to the Morton F. Acropolis Savings and Loan Association of Chicago. Then you'll find out."

Chapter 8

And so the next morning, right after breakfast, my dad, my Grandma Leah, my Great-Grandpa Maurice, and I all got into a **cab** and went to the Morton F. Acropolis Savings and **Loan Association** of Chicago.

At first the bank **officer** we spoke with told us she couldn't find any secret bank **account bear**ing the number Maurice had given us.

"Tell her to look harder," said Maurice from inside the cat **carrier**.

The bank officer looked **startle**d.

"Please look harder, ma'am," I said.

And so the bank officer looked harder.

"You'd better be telling us the truth about this," I said to the cat carrier.

"Don't be so **mistrust**ful," said the voice from inside the cat carrier.

The bank officer returned.

"I did find something," she said. "An account was opened a great many years ago. I don't know if it's the right one. But it does bear the same number you gave me."

"What's the name on the account?" I asked.

"That, of course, would be a secret," said the bank officer.

"What if I told you the first name?" I said. "Would you just **nod** your head if I'm right?"

"What name are you thinking of?" she asked.

"Maurice," I said.

The bank officer nodded.

"I'm right!" I said. Great-Grandpa Maurice was telling the truth! "Now how do we get the money?"

"Well, the **individual** whose name is on the account would have to **sign** for it," she said.

We all looked at each other.

"What if he couldn't do that?" asked my

dad.

"Why couldn't he do that?" said the bank officer.

"What if he were . . . What if something had happened to him?" I said.

"Such as what?" said the bank officer.

"Such as, oh, I don't know, such as he turned into a cat," I said.

"Such as he *died,*" said my dad quickly.

"Well, if the account holder is **decease**d," said the bank officer, "then the money would go into **probate**. Probate is a very long, very **complicate**d **legal process**. It takes years to **sort out**."

"What does deceased mean?" I **whisper**ed.

"Dead," said the voice inside the cat

carrier.

"What if he **turn**ed **into** a cat?" I asked.

"Excuse me?" said the bank officer.

My dad looked at me and shook his head.

"Do you believe in **reincarnation**?" I asked the bank officer.

"No," she said.

We all looked at each other. We didn't have any idea what to do next.

"Hey," said the voice in the cat carrier, "can I talk to her?"

"Is there somebody inside that animal carrier?" asked the bank officer, **alarm**ed.

"Hey, let me out of here!" said the voice.

I looked at my dad. He **shrug**ged. I

opened the cat carrier. Great-Grandpa Maurice **hop**ped out onto the **counter**.

"Uh, I'm afraid **pet**s aren't allowed inside the bank," said the bank officer, "The **regulation**s **specific**ally **forbid**—"

"Oh, **pipe down** a minute, sis,[1]" said Great-Grandpa Maurice. "And maybe we can **clear** this **up**."

The bank officer looked like she might **faint**.

"This," I said, "is my great-grandfather, Maurice. He opened the account with your bank many years ago when he was still a person."

The bank officer **lean**ed heavily against

---

1 **sis** 젊은 여자를 부르는 비격식적인 호칭.

the counter so she wouldn't fall down.

"This individual does, indeed, appear to be . . . a cat," she whispered.

"You're darned tootin'[2] I am," said Great-Grandpa Maurice. "And if you don't mind, I'd like to **withdraw** all the money in my account and give it to my family."

"Are you able to . . . sign for it?" she whispered, **barely** able to speak.

"Hey, dollface,[3]" he said, "I'm a cat. Maybe you **notice**d. I don't happen to have an **opposable thumb**.[4] So I can't hold a pen."

---

2 **darned tootin'** 다른 사람의 말에 동의할 때 사용하는 속어.

3 **dollface** 보통 젊은 여자나 어린아이를 부를 때 쓰는 호칭.

4 **opposable thumb** 인간이나 침팬지 등 영장류의 특징으로 다른 네 손가락과 마주 보는 엄지손가락을 의미한다. 단순히 물건을 잡는 일도 이런 엄지손가락이 있어서 가능하다.

"If you're unable to sign," she whispered, "we would be unable to . . . give you the money."

"Why the heck[5] not?" he asked.

"It would not be . . . **consistent** with company **policy**," she whispered, her eyes now **squeeze**d shut.

"Then how's about changing company policy?" he said. "From now on, anytime somebody gets reincarnated as a cat and comes in to get his money, all he has to do is ask for it. What do you say?"

The bank officer took a deep breath.

"I just don't . . . know if we can do that," she said.

---

5 **heck** '도대체', '젠장' 또는 '제기랄'이라는 뜻으로 당혹스럽거나 짜증스러운 감정을 강조하는 속어.

"OK then, get me Morty," said Great-Grandpa Maurice.

"Who's Morty?" asked the bank officer.

"Who's Morty?" repeated Great-Grandpa Maurice. "You mean to say you don't know Morton F. Acropolis, the **found**er of the bank?"

And with that, the cat **leap**t off the counter and **hotfoot**ed **it** down the **hall**.

"Now just a minute there," the bank officer called after him. "I can't let you—"

Great-Grandpa Maurice stopped in front of a **fancy** door. It said "Morton F. Acropolis" on the front.

"Hey, Morty!" **yell**ed Great-Grandpa Maurice. "You in there?"

"Maurice?" called a surprised voice

from inside the office. "Maurice, is that you?"

The cat pushed the founder's door open with his nose and walked inside. My dad, Grandma Leah, and I followed close behind. The bank officer came right after us.

Behind a long desk that looked like some kind of **antique** sat the oldest man I had ever seen. He was also one of the shortest. I **doubt** if he was a lot taller than me, and he had on a pair of glasses with **amazing**ly thick lenses.

"Hey, Morty, great to see you!" said the cat.

"Maurice, you old dog,[6] is that you?" cried Mr. Acropolis. He **squint**ed through

Morton F. Acropolis
Founder

his glasses and **peer**ed over the top of his desk. "My eyes aren't what they used to be. But I'd **recognize** that voice anywhere, even after all these years!"

"So how have you been, Morty?"

"**Never mind** me, what about you, Maurice? I heard you were dead."

"I was," said the cat. "But I'm better now. Listen, Morty, I got a problem. Maybe you can help me."

"For you, Maurice? Anything. What can I do?"

"Sir," said the bank officer, "do you **realize** you're talking to a c—"

"Quiet, Lola," **snap**ped the old man. "I

---

6 **dog** 남자를 가리키는 속어로 '녀석', '놈'이라는 뜻.

haven't seen this man in ages."

"But he's not a man, sir," said the bank officer, "he's a c—"

"Quiet!" shouted Mr. Acropolis. "Go ahead, Maurice, what can I do for you?"

"It's the money I made on the hot dog sweater, Morty. I'd like to withdraw it from my account. But this young lady here tells me I can't."

"**Poppycock**!" **roar**ed Mr. Acropolis. "I **invest**ed in that hot dog sweater myself. Smartest move I ever made. Give the man his money, Lola!"

"But, Mr. Acropolis, he's unable to sign for it."

"Why's that?"

"He can't hold a pen in his **paws**," she

said.

"Well, I can't hold a pen in *my* paws either," said Mr. Acropolis. "A man gets to be our age, **dear**, there are certain things he can't do by himself any longer. Help him, for the love of Pete![7]"

"Y-yes, sir," said the bank officer.

And so we all walked out of Mr. Acropolis's office. Then, with shaking hands, the bank officer put a pen between the cat's paws and helped him sign his name. Then she wrote out a check and handed it to us. My dad looked at the amount and **whistle**d.

"Maurice, I thought you said there was

---

7 **for the love of Pete** '제발', '부디'라는 뜻으로 간청하거나 애원할 때 쓰는 표현.

thirty thousand dollars in this account," he said.

"How much is in there?" asked Maurice.

"Closer to ninety," said my dad.

"Ninety thousand dollars?" asked Grandma Leah. It was the first thing she'd said since we'd arrived at the bank.

"Well, that's after more than thirty years of **interest**," said my dad.

"And you really want us to have this?" I asked.

"On one **condition**," said Maurice.

"What's that?"

"That you leave me enough for a first-class, one-way ticket to Palm Beach,[8] and a few years' **rent** in a **deluxe** pet hotel, with a

standing order for herring and sour cream every morning, and a glass of schnapps every night."

"You're not going to live with us?" I said.

"As much as I love you, Zack," said Maurice, "I've always wanted to spend my **golden years** in Florida. I understand there are **folk**s down there who might be **willing** to invest a few dollars in **invent**ions of a somewhat **speculative nature**."

So Maurice went off to live the good life in Florida. But before he did he had the bank

---

8 **Palm Beach** 팜비치. 미국 플로리다주(州)의 남동부에 있는 도시. 겨울철 휴양을 위해 많이 찾는 곳이다.

officer open his safe-**deposit** box.[9] There it was. A baseball signed by Lou Gehrig, Ty Cobb, and Rogers Hornsby.

"This is for you, kid," he said to me. "I was going to keep it, but hey, what the heck does an old **pussycat** need with an old baseball anyway?"

Even though Great-Grandpa Maurice was kind of **pushy**, I was really sad to see him go.

"Hey, Zack," he said, "**cheer up**. Now you can go back to the animal **shelter** and get that little tuxedo **kitten** you were looking at."

"But you said he has **flea**s and **worm**s

---

9 **safe-deposit box** 은행에서 귀중품 보관을 위해 개인에게 대여해 주는 안전 금고.

and never learned how to use a **litter** box," I replied.

"Maybe so," he said. "But there's one thing about him that might make you **overlook** all that."

"What?"

"In a **former** life he was Babe Ruth.[10]"

---

10 Babe Ruth 베이브 루스. 본명은 조지 허먼 루스(George Herman Ruth)로 미국에서 가장 인기가 많았던 프로 야구 선수이자 메이저리그를 대표하는 홈런 타자이다.